Beckett
IN 90 MINUTES

Paul Strathern

IVAN R. DEE
CHICAGO

www.ivanrdee.com

Library of Congress Cataloging-in-Publication Data:
Strathern, Paul, 1940–
    Beckett in 90 minutes / Paul Strathern.
        p. cm. — (Great writers in 90 minutes)
    ISBN 1-56663-585-3 (cloth : alk. paper) —
    ISBN 1-56663-586-1 (pbk. : alk. paper)
    1. Beckett, Samuel, 1906– 2. Authors, Irish—20th century—Biography. 3. Authors, French—20th century—Biography. I. Title: Beckett in ninety minutes. II. Title.

PR6003.E282Z8356 2005
848'.914099aB—dc22
                                                2004056920

Contents

BECKETT IN 90 MINUTES

Introduction

In 1946, Beckett found himself back in Ireland, staying with his disapproving mother. He had left Paris because he did not have enough money to continue living in his chosen city. He was now approaching forty, and forced to confront the prospect of his utter failure. All the hopes of his brilliant youth had come to nothing. Apart from a few scattered pieces, mostly in small magazines, he had published just one novel. This had passed virtually unnoticed by the reading public, the bulk of its copies being remaindered. During the war he had written another novel and had at last felt that he was getting somewhere. But this novel had recently been turned down by his publishers, who had reacted to it with "considerable bewilderment," finding it "wild and unintelligible." In their opinion it stood no chance whatsoever of publication.

Though deeply wounded by this rejection, Beckett too was dissatisfied with his work. He disagreed with his publisher's rejection, but he felt a nagging suspicion that he was somehow not on the right track. Something was missing, something eluded him, preventing him from achieving all of which he felt he was capable. The great promise he had shown, the promise that had been recognized by no less than James Joyce himself, remained unfulfilled.

Beckett was at a loss over what to do, and he began drinking heavily in the bars of Dublin. At night he would wander the streets in a bemused state, lost in his thoughts. One night he found himself standing at the end of the stone pier of Dun Laoghaire harbor. Years later he would recall this moment in an early version of his play *Krapp's Last Tape*, where Krapp's recorded voice disjointedly relates:

Intellectually a year of profound gloom and indigence until that memorable night in March, at the end of the pier, in the howling wind, never to be forgotten, when suddenly I saw the whole thing. The turning point at last. This I imagine is what I have chiefly to set down this evening against the day when my work will be done and perhaps no place left in my memory and no thankfulness for the miracle that—for the fire it set alight. What I saw then was that the assumption I had been going on all my life, namely . . . clear to me at last that the dark I have been fighting off all this time is in reality my most . . . unshatterable association till my dying day of story and night with the light of understanding and . . .

Beckett had realized that he had been looking in the wrong place, in the wrong direction. Instead of trying to come to terms with the world around him, he should have been focusing on the inner world, on "the dark he had struggled to keep under." Joyce had gone as far as it was possible to go "in the direction of knowing more, [being] in control of one's material." But Beckett "realized that my own way was in impoverishment, in lack of knowledge and in taking away, in subtracting rather than adding." His subject matter was not the great intellectual achievements of the human condition but its hopelessness and despair, the grim farcical element of its inescapable failure, all the things that he himself knew so well. From this point on, Beckett would no longer care whether what he wrote appeared "wild and unintelligible." He would express the disconnectedness of his own inner voice, the voice that had accompanied him through the long voyage of his life so far.

Beckett's Life and Works

Samuel Beckett was born on Good Friday, April 13, 1906, in Foxrock, a middle-class suburb between the Wicklow Mountains and the Irish Sea south of Dublin. His family was descended from Huguenots, the Protestants who were forced to flee Catholic persecution in France during the late eighteenth century. But the Becketts had long since lost any awareness of themselves as anything other than Irish. The family was part of the prosperous Protestant minority in Ireland, which at the time was still part of Great Britain. There is little evidence of creative inclination among Beckett's predecessors, with the possible exception of his paternal grandmother Fannie, whose

7

unfulfilled sensitivity drove her to drink. According to family mythology, she would lock herself in her room for days on end; at other times she sported a parrot on her shoulder, which would screech with jealous rage when anyone kissed Fannie.

William Beckett, the writer's father, was a jovial philistine who made a considerable fortune as a building contractor and property speculator. Beckett retained affectionate memories of his father, with whom he would go on long walks over the barren, treeless countryside of the nearby Wicklow Mountains. But the dominant parent in Beckett's life was his mother May, a tall, long-faced, difficult woman, descended from an impecunious landowning family. All who met her agree that there was something odd about her, something that didn't quite fit in with the role of conventional suburban life. She suffered from insomnia, and had the carpets removed from the upstairs floors so that she could hear the footfall of any approaching ghost. Despite this, there was little overtly eccentric about her, apart from her willfulness. This appears to have met its match in her second son Samuel. Beckett's older brother Frank took after his father, but it soon became clear that Sam was psychologically much more complex, a condition he appeared to find as irksome as everyone else. As a result, he was a solitary child, both by circumstance and inclination.

Surprisingly, the reserved young Beckett did well at school, being both intellectually gifted and accomplished at sports despite his bad eyesight. From an early age he had been forced to wear round, steel-rimmed spectacles, which he would continue to wear all his life. In 1920, at the age of fourteen, he became a border at Portora Royal School, a Protestant private school in the province of Ulster, which was to become Northern Ireland. In 1922 Ireland gained independence, with Northern Ireland electing to remain part of Britain. There followed a civil war in the Irish Free State between the two Catholic factions. The schoolboy Beckett would have been largely insulated from all this but would certainly have been aware of the upheavals that were taking place. It is difficult to judge the precise effect of this traumatic historical background: it would certainly leave a profound mark upon his Protestant Irish contemporary, the painter Francis Bacon.

The newly independent Ireland was a troubled, desperately poor country, heavily dominated by the Catholic church, which forbad contraception. As a result, large families contributed further to the poverty of the majority Catholic population. Out of ambition or necessity, many emigrated to Britain and America, leaving saddened abandoned families behind. Although Beckett never lived in poverty in his homeland, the hopeless downtrodden characters who inhabit much of his later fiction would have been recognizable on any street in Dublin—even if the background Beckett gave them was often more reminiscent of the Wicklow Mountains. Beckett's unaccommodated man may have had a distant literary ancestor in the the "poor, bare, forked animal" seen by Shakespeare's King Lear on the blasted heath, but the characters in Beckett's work also mirrored real people, whose "hopeless" temperament and grim humor had been forged by real despair.

At the age of seventeen Beckett went to Trinity College, Dublin, where he studied modern languages (English, French, and Italian). Here he quickly acquired the seemingly obligatory penchant for vast quantities of Guinness and an equally unquenchable thirst for literature and philosophy. In his final fourth year he won a place on the university cricket team, which went on a short summer tour playing against English counties. (These matches are recorded in Wisden, the cricketers' bible, making him the only Nobel Prize–winner to appear in its august pages.)

In his final exams, Beckett won the gold medal as the top scholar. He emerged from university an awkward young man, who in that scornful but telling Dublin phrase was "educated beyond his intelligence." Like his philosophical hero Descartes, he found it difficult to rise from his bed before noon. This made him particularly unsuited to the employment he now gained as a schoolmaster at Campbell College, Belfast, a middle-class Ulster institution similar to Portora. As with many a brilliant student, he quickly acquired a distaste for the amiable dullards who formed the staff and pupils; to them, he appeared a conceited and arrogant young man. The final straw came when he was summoned yet again to appear before the exasperated headmaster, who forcefully reminded him that the pupils he treated with such contempt were in fact "the cream of Ulster." "Yes," replied Beckett, "rich and thick." He found himself on the next train to Dublin. The only surprise was that he had lasted as long as two terms.

Fortunately his linguistic success at Trinity College enabled him to qualify for an exchange post as *lecteur* at the prestigious French École Normale Supérieure. This would allow him to live for two years in Paris. Nothing could have suited Beckett better. Within months he had taken up residence in a small room on the Left Bank and was wearing a beret, his fingers browned with nicotine stains from strong Galois tobacco, drinking copious amounts of cheap red wine in the bars of the Latin Quarter. Although he duly carried out his light tutorial duties at the École, he appears to have mixed little with the students, among whom he might have encountered Jean-Paul Sartre and Simone de Beauvoir, who were currently the top philosophy students. Instead Beckett met James Joyce, who had published *Ulysses* just six years earlier and already had a reputation in some circles as Ireland's finest modern writer. The brilliant and impressionable young Beckett was overwhelmed by the brilliant and manipulative Joyce, who soon had Beckett running errands and doing secretarial chores.

In 1929, Beckett contributed an essay to a book celebrating Joyce's work, and embarked upon a translation into French of a section from *Finnegans Wake*, Joyce's work in progress. Beckett even assisted Joyce in the composition of this difficult modernistic work, taking down the author's words as he dictated. This task would result in a characteristic episode. On one occasion when Beckett read back to Joyce the passage he had just dictated, the flow of densely allusive Joycean prose was found to include the words "come in," which Joyce could not remember saying. After some puzzled discussion, Joyce recalled that at one point someone had knocked on the door, and he must have replied, "Come in."

This amused Joyce so much that he decided to leave Beckett's copy intact. Such accidents fell easily into the prose of *Finnegans Wake*:

> Not a sound falling. Lispn! No wind no word. Only a leaf, just a leaf and the leaves. The woods are fond always. As were we their babes in. And robins in crews so. It is for me goolden wending. Unless? Away! Rise up, man of the hooths, you have slept so long! Or is it only so mesleems?

At the time this was the pinnacle of modernistic prose. The young overintellectual Beckett was entranced by its richness of literary allusion. Here was something he could not fail to admire, something that perhaps one day he might seek to emulate.

Despite his shyness, Beckett was by now an attractive young man. Joyce's emotionally unstable daughter Lucia soon fell in love with the tall, taciturn figure who regularly called at the Joyce apartment. Beckett did his best to discourage her, but this disturbing episode appears to have contributed to her eventual mental collapse some years later. It also resulted in a brief estrangment with Joyce, though his influence on Beckett's way of thinking remained as strong as ever. Beckett now had ambitions to become a writer, and began composing poetry. It was highly allusive, in the Joycean manner, with obscure references to all manner of writers in various languages.

In 1930 the shipping heiress Nancy Cunard sponsored a prize for a poem of less than a hundred lines on the subject of time. Beckett heard of this prize only on the evening before the deadline for entries, whereupon he stayed up till 3 a.m. writing a poem called *Whoroscope*, based very obliquely on the life of Descartes. It opens:

What's that?
An egg?
By the brothers Boot it stinks fresh.
Give it to Gillot.

The pages of notes at the end of the poem explain how Descartes "liked his omelette made from eggs hatched from eight to ten days," that "In 1640 the brothers Boot refuted Aristotle in Dublin," and how "Descartes passed on the

15

easier problems in analytical geometry to his valet Gillot." *Whoroscope* goes on like this for ninety-eight lines, stuffed with reference yet empty of coherence, meaningful to the point of meaninglessness. This combination of conceit, erudition, obscurity, and fashionable modernity won Nancy Cunard's prize and was duly published in book form by her Hours Press.

Despite this minor success, Beckett remained a distinctly solitary individual, beset by an increasingly profound psychological bewilderment, resulting in bouts of depression and deep suffering. It was around this time that he discovered the misanthropic nineteenth-century German philosopher Schopenhauer, whose works are imbued with a deep pessimism. According to Schopenhauer, the world is merely representation, an illusory veil of Maya sustained by an evil Will. Beckett found himself drawn to what he called Schopenahuer's "intellectual justification of unhappiness." Spiritual suffering was the lot of humanity: it should be accepted as such, not dismissed as some kind of psychological failing. Later Beckett would write that the experience of discovering Schopenhauer was "Like suddenly a window opened in a fog."

By 1930, Beckett's time as a *lecteur* at the École Normale Supérieur was over, and he was forced to return to Dublin. Here he reluctantly took a post as a lecturer at his alma mater, Trinity College. By now friends had brought Beckett to the attention of a London publisher, who had commissioned him to write another work on time. This was to be a critical monologue on Proust, the author of the vast seven-volume novel *Remembrance of Things Past*. Beckett's monograph is pervaded by Schopenhauerian gloom: "There is no escape from yesterday because yesterday has deformed us, or been deformed by us." Yet amidst his displays of erudition and his attempts to come to terms with the great French writer, Beckett manages to focus his language into a number of pithy epigrams. "Reality, whether approached imaginatively or empirically, remains a surface, hermetic." "For Proust, as for the painter, style is more a question of vision than of technique." More pertinently, if more obliquely, *Proust* also evolved into an attempt by Beckett to set down his own ideas about writing.

> Tragedy is not concerned with human justice. Tragedy is the statement of an expiation, but not the miserable expiation of a codified breach of a local arrangement, organized by the knaves for the fools. The tragic figure represents the expiation of original sin, of the original and eternal sin . . . the sin of having been born.

After just four terms of teaching at Trinity College, Beckett found that he was unable to go on. Despite his deep academic knowledge, he knew that the world of academia was not for him. To the consternation of his parents and his supportive colleagues, he resigned. He was now twenty-six years old, increasingly beset by depression, and virtually incapable of holding down any kind of job. His mother nagged, his father bluffly tried to snap him out of it. He began drinking heavily; his parents gave him some money and he returned to Paris, where he began writing a novel. This would eventually become *A*

Dream of Fair to Middling Women. Its protago-
nist is a character called Belacqua, named after
the character in Dante's *Divine Comedy* who is
sent to Purgatory for the sin of sloth. The novel
is loosely based on various incidents in Beckett's
life, and Belacqua is recognizably Beckett himself. It consists of several episodes, interspersed
with occasional intellectual meanderings. In the
end, Beckett himself was forced to admit that the
novel was a failure, though he would eventually
salvage one section as a short story called "Dante
and the Lobster." In its depiction of Belacqua's
physical decrepitude and mental inconsistency
this story contains the first inkling of some of the
themes that would come to fruition in Beckett's
later work. There is also the occasional glimpse
of Beckett's grim, farcical humor, as for instance
in: "His aunt was in the garden tending whatever
flowers die at that time of year."

In 1933, Beckett's father died, leaving him a
small but regular income, just enough for him to
live on. He began a period of several months
wandering about Europe, traveling through Germany and France, living in cheap lodgings,

mooching about various cities, and visiting art galleries. In between times he wrote a number of short stories and poems. His letters to his friends reveal him by turns depressed and ebulliently defiant. (His comments on the literary world that rejected his works would always tend to the latter. Critics were referred to as "chartered recountants"; the well-known London publisher Chatto and Windus became "Shaton and Wind-up.") Outwardly he became ever more withdrawn.

Beckett ended up in London, where he settled in a cheap room in Chelsea, in the district appropriately known as World's End. Here he embarked upon a period of psychoanalysis, part of which involved attending, along with his psychiatrist, a lecture by Jung. During the course of the lecture, Jung explained how there is no unity to consciousness, which is capable of splitting into separate complexes, each of which can develop its own ego, to the point where "They speak in voices which are like the voices of definite people." At one stage Jung compared the mind to a series of spheres, one within the other, each be-

coming darker, with the darkest at the very heart
of the mind, containing the personal and collec-
tive unconscious. When the mind relinquished its
conscious autonomy, the unconscious grew in
strength until it overcame the conscious mind.
Then the individual became "the victim of a new
autonomous activity that does not start from his
ego but starts from the dark sphere." These interpretations were to have a profound and last-
ing effect on Beckett, but none more so than
Jung's assertion that there are certain people who
suffer from the fact that they have "never been
really born." Beckett would continue to identify
with this diagnosis, until finally it became an in-
tegral element of his most profound work.

Beckett later remarked, "I hated London."
He felt alienated and alone. His accent marked
him out as an Irishman, and consequent preju-
dice, while he found himself unable to relate to
English literary acquaintances. Eventually, after
"two bad years," he decided it was "time to pull
the plug on London." He returned to Ireland to
live with his mother—who ironically had been

one of the main reasons for him going into psychoanalysis. Their relationship was too close and too difficult. Her overbearing character and utter disregard for his ambitions to become a writer left him exhausted and bewildered, yet unable finally to break free.

In between times Beckett continued writing poetry and short stories. In 1933 his book of short stories entitled *More Pricks Than Kicks* was accepted by a London publisher. This book consisted of a number of linked stories featuring Belacqua, the hero of his abandoned novel.

My sometime friend Belacqua enlivened the last phase of his solipsism, before he toed the line and began to relish the world, with the belief that the best thing he had to do was to move constantly from place to place. He did not know how this conclusion had been gained, but that it was not thanks to his preferring one place to another he felt sure.

A year later a friend in Paris offered to publish his collection of poems, *Echo's Bones and Other*

Precipitates, as long as Beckett contributed toward the cost. The title poem, in its entirety, runs:

> asylum under my tread all this day
> their muffled revels as the flesh falls
> breaking without fear or favor wind
> the gantelope of sense and nonsense run
> taken by the maggots for what they are

Such poetry, published in a small limited edition in English, in Paris, attracted little attention. Beckett was now almost thirty, and still having to live off his wits and his small private income.

He settled down to have another go at writing a novel. Between writing and rewriting, this would take him three years to complete, finally being accepted by a London publisher in 1937. This is recognizably Beckett's first accomplished, post-apprentice work. The author's need to inflict his great erudition upon the reader is restrained, to the point where the proceedings remain more or less comprehensible. The bleak, self-defensive humor comes into its own, and the result is a work by turns farcical and philosophical, surely the work of a truly oblique and original mind beginning to express itself with a measure of confidence rather than arrogance. Its opening words set the tone:

> The sun shone, having no alternative, on the nothing new. Murphy sat out of it, as though he were free, in a mew in West Brompton. Here for what might have been six months he had eaten, drunk, slept, and put his clothes on and off, in a medium-sized cage of northwestern aspect commanding an unbroken view of medium-sized cages of south-eastern aspect.

Murphy is an impecunious Irish intellectual driven to misanthropic despair as he seeks some form of spiritual relief from the world around him. We see him sitting in his room, naked and bound to a rocking chair:

> Only the most local movements were possible. Sweat poured off him, tightening the thongs. The breath was not perceptible. The eyes, cold and unwavering as a gull's, stared up. . . .

Murphy subjected himself to this ordeal because it gave him pleasure:

> First it gave his body pleasure, it appeased his body. Then it set him free in his mind. For it was not until his body was appeased that he could come alive in his mind. . . .

Murphy has affinities with many of Beckett's favorite thinkers. Like Descartes, thinking is his proof to himself of his existence, and his philosophy leads him to believe that his mind is separate from his body. He is possessed by a Schopenhauerian pessimism and views the world as a veil of maya. And besides witty echoes of various philosophers, there are also direct references to Jung:

> Murphy's mind pictured itself as a large hollow sphere, hermetically closed to the universe without. This was not an impoverishment, for it excluded nothing that it did not itself contain. Nothing ever had been, was, or would be in the universe outside it but was already present as virtual, or

actual, or virtual rising into actual, or actual falling into virtual, in the universe inside it.

Despite his solipsistic inclinations, Murphy cannot avoid becoming embroiled in the outside world. In the course of the novel we meet the prostitute Celia, who is Murphy's sole support, until he ends up in an asylum called the Magdalen Mental Mercyseat. Here he continues his search for Nirvana, rocking in his chair, until someone inadvertently pulls the wrong chain in the lavatory, releasing gas into his room, where there is a lighted candle. After the fatal explosion, we learn of Murphy's will: "With regard to the disposal of these my body, mind, and soul, I desire that they be burnt and placed in a paper bag." His ashes are then to be taken to the Abbey Theatre in Dublin, where they are to be tipped down the lavatory, "and I desire that the chain be there pulled upon them, if possible during the performance." Unfortunately the man chosen to execute this task, his friend Cooper, gets drunk in a bar and ends up angrily throwing the paper bag containing Murphy's ashes "at a man who had given him great offense." The bag bursts, scattering the ashes:

> By closing time the body, mind, and soul of Murphy were freely distributed over the floor of the saloon; and before another dayspring greyened the earth had been swept away with the sand, the beer, the butts, the glass, the matches, the spits, the vomit.

Unsurprisingly, the publication of such an oddity passed all but unnoticed in literary London. But the little attention it did eventually attract was significant. Dylan Thomas wrote an unfavorable review but declared, "Murphy is the individual ostrich in the mass-produced desert," characterizing Beckett's humor as "Freudian blarney: Sodom and Begorrah." Later the young Anglo-Irish Iris Murdoch, more than a decade before she became a writer, found a deep rapport with Murphy's Irishness and originality. Later still, an unread copy was borrowed from a public library by the penniless actor Harold Pinter, who was so overwhelmed that he decided to steal it.

Meanwhile Beckett's life in Ireland was going from bad to worse. He was still living at home but spent the afternoons and evenings wandering the pubs of Dublin. Mornings consisted of hangovers and motherly reprimands. He began to develop psychosomatic illnesses, suffering particularly from scrofulous rashes, anal cysts, and boils. By the autumn of 1937, illness-inflicted abstinence allowed him to pay off his accumulated pub debts, and he had enough money to travel again. He set off for Paris, determined that this time he would stay away as long as he could.

Unfortunately he was called back to Dublin to appear in a libel case, which one of his drinking companions had taken against the writer Oliver St. John Gogarty. Loyally Beckett returned, but his public appearance in court proved traumatic. Squirming in the limelight of the witness box, Beckett was forced to endure a humiliating vilification of his character by Gogarty's counsel. Adopting an air of bluff puritanical philistinism, the lawyer mercilessly played to the gallery. Beckett was dismissed as a pretentious intellectual, the writer of a pornographic poem "by the title of Horoscope with the capital 'W' prefixed." Next day a report in the *Irish Times* referred to Beckett as "the bawd and blasphemer from Paris." He didn't dare go home and face his mother. This time Beckett left Ireland swearing never to return.

Back in Paris he found himself unable to concentrate on serious writing and was pleased to take on occasional literary hackwork for extra funds. Word that he had now published a novel began to spread among his friends. He made contact with James Joyce and through other friends was invited to one of the wild parties thrown by the American heiress Peggy Guggenheim, who was in Paris buying up modern art for her London gallery. Guggenheim described Beckett as:

. . . a tall, lanky Irishman of about thirty with enormous green eyes that never looked at you. He wore spectacles and always seemed to be far away solving some intellectual problem; he spoke very seldom and never said anything stupid. He was excessively polite, but rather awkward. He dressed badly in tight-fitting French clothes and had no vanity about his appearance.

Guggenheim soon fell in love with Beckett, and they began an on-and-off affair that would last many months. But in the end the vivacious, socializing Guggenheim, who collected famous names as much as she collected paintings, and the elusive misanthropic Beckett, proved incompatible, and they went their separate ways. Decades later, in her autobiography *Confessions of an Art Addict*, Peggy Guggenheim would claim that among the many famous figures she had enountered, only three immediately struck her as geniuses—the surrealist Max Ernst, the sculptor Alberto Giacometti, and Samuel Beckett. This was apparently not hindsight. In her own words, when she had first met Beckett he had been merely "a frustrated writer, a pure intellectual," but despite their difficulties and their disparate attitudes she had detected in him an exceptional creative spark, a spark that Beckett himself was far from sure he possessed at the time. Joyce too claimed to see this. Others believed in Beckett, even when he did not believe in himself—though it would still be many years before such faith was justified.

Meanwhile the heavy drinking continued. *Un ballon rouge* drunk at the zinc counter of a small Paris café cost little more than a box of matches, and Beckett would regularly end up making the rounds of the late-night cafés in Montparnasse, where he now lived. Despite his hectic nightlife, he still found time for exercise, playing occasional games of tennis with expatriate friends who invited him to a private club on the outskirts of Paris. For mixed doubles he was occasionally partnered by a talented French pianist called Suzanne Deschevaux-Dumesnil. It was also at this time that Beckett formed a close friendship with the Swiss-Italian sculptor Alberto Giacometti, who shared Beckett's solitariness, fondness for late-night bars, and sardonic view of the world. The two insomniacs would share long understanding silences at the bar, pondering the evils of the world between draining their glasses. Giacometti had an unabashed penchant for prostitutes, and Beckett appears to have joined him in this pursuit as well as exploring the field on his own. Almost certainly as a result of this, Beckett became involved in an incident in Montparnasse late one night in January 1938. In the course of an argument with a pimp who appeared to know him, and wanted to borrow some money, Beckett was stabbed in the chest. He fell to the ground and was quickly rushed to the hospital. Here it was found that the knife blade had barely missed his heart and lung. He was lucky to be alive.

Beckett had long been prone to hypochondria, but now that the affliction was both genuine and serious he behaved stoically. When news of Beckett's injury reached Dublin, his mother and brother immediately set off on the quickest route to Paris, which in those days involved a gruelling twenty-fours hours of continuous traveling, including two ferry crossings and three rail journeys. Beckett was deeply moved by his mother's evident concern, and they appear to have affected an awkward reconciliation. The events had a deep effect upon Beckett and even broke his writer's block. In his hospital bed he found himself writing poetry again.

Another hospital visitor was Beckett's tennis partner Suzanne. Although she was thirty-eight and thus six years older than Beckett, it quickly became clear that she was attracted to him. When Beckett left the hospital they began going out together. They made an unlikely couple: he drank, she did not; he lived a bohemian life, she preferred lace-making. But they quickly discovered a mutual interest in classical music and the arts; in time they became lovers. Unlike Peggy Guggenheim, however, Suzanne appeared to have a more calming effect on Beckett. As Peggy Guggenheim cattily remarked about Suzanne: "She made curtains while I made scenes."

In the summer of 1939, Beckett received the royalties he was due from the publication of *Murphy* and traveled to Ireland to see his mother. During the visit, Britain and France declared war on Germany, plunging Europe into World War II. Ireland remained neutral, but to the consternation of his mother, Beckett insisted upon returning to Paris, telling her, "I promised so many friends that I would be back."

By now Beckett and Suzanne were living together in a small flat on the Rue des Favourites, a grim, featureless street south of Montparnasse. In the spring of 1940 the Germans invaded France, quickly approaching Paris. Beckett and Suzanne fled with thousands of refugees who headed south, but eventually made their way back to German-occupied Paris. Beckett had no wish to return to Ireland, and Suzanne was equally reluctant to return to live with her parents in provincial Troyes. Back in Paris, Beckett soon joined a resistance network. With characteristic diffidence, and more than a little truth, he later characterized his actions as "Boy Scout stuff." But there is no doubting the fact that this involved real danger. (After the war, Beckett would be awarded the Croix de Guerre for his efforts, though he typically omitted to tell anyone of this for many years.) In 1942 the Germans penetrated the resistance cell with which Beckett was involved. He and Suzanne immediately left the Rue des Favourites and went on the run. After being put up at various secret addresses in Paris, they set off south with false papers for un-occupied Vichy France, which was run by Petain's collaborationist government. For days they tramped the roads, sometimes in despair, of-ten bickering in their extremity. Elements of this dialogue would later surface in the absurd ex-changes between Vladmir and Estragon in Beck-ett's *Waiting for Godot.*

ESTRAGON: I can't go on like this.
VLADIMIR: That's what you think.
. . . .
VLADIMIR: Well, shall we go?
ESTRAGON: Yes, let's go.
They do not move.

Eventually Beckett and Suzanne reached the remote village of Rousillon in the craggy hills above the Rhone delta, some four hundred miles south of Paris. Here they hid out for the re-mainder of the war, doing occasional farm work to help pay for their keep. Beckett would some-times join the local Maquis (resistance) on armed night patrols. These were largely futile exercises involving twenty-mile hikes across rugged heathland, intended to bolster morale. Beckett soon fell into deep dejection, but attempted to keep up his spirits by beginning a novel, which would eventually be called *Watt*, his first sustained creative work in more than five years.

Watt would mark a break from Beckett's previous work. Gone is the self-conscious intellectualism, the tendency to pretentious superiority. In its place comes a distinctly neurotic sense of futility as Beckett attempts to explore and embody various philosophical questions in concrete form. This is achieved by what would become a distinctly Beckett-like form of reductionism, which besides reducing the narrative to its bare bones also involves a *reductio ad absurdum* of the entire novelistic genre.

In one sense *Watt* marks a serious deepening of Beckett's psychological affinities. Previously, Murphy had shown deep empathy with the schizophrenics in the Mercyseat asylum. In the case of *Watt*, the eponymous hero unmistakably *is* schizophrenic, both in his actions and in the obsessive way in which his story is recounted. We are introduced to Watt in slapstick fashion:

> Watt bumped into a porter wheeling a milk-can. Watt fell and his hat and bags were scattered. The porter did not fall, but he let go his can, which fell back with a thump on its tilted rim, rocked rattling on its base and finally came to a stand. This was a happy chance, for had it fallen on its side . . .

In basic outline the story has a symbolic, distinctly Kafkaesque simplicity. After a series of tragi-farcical mishaps, the bedraggled Watt turns up at the house of Mr. Knott, where he is to work as a servant. After being subjected to a seemingly endless diatribe by the departing servant he is replacing, Watt takes up his duties on the ground floor, performing his allotted menial tasks. Eventually he graduates to the top of the house where he looks after the bedroom, taking the place of Erskine, whose employment has come to an end. During his time in the house, Watt's life revolves around the mysterious but elusive Mr. Knott, the master of the house. "Mr.

Knott saw nobody, heard from nobody, as far as Watt could see. But Watt was not so foolish as to draw any conclusion from this." The latter observation is the key to Watt's overriding philosophical attitude toward the world. Watt catches a few glimpses of Mr. Knott, the most notable being of him meditating in the garden. Otherwise Mr. Knott remains unknown, seemingly defined only by negation.

The narrative of the story is characterized by neurotic obsession with detail and repetition. This comes across as perverse, psychotic, or humorous—depending upon one's attitude toward the repetitive goings-on in which Watt becomes involved. At first these appear trivial to the point of tediousness, but they soon open up into a world of deeper meaning:

> What distressed Watt in this incident . . . and in subsequent similar incidents, was not so much that he did not know what had happened, for he did not care what had happened, as that nothing had happened, that a thing that was nothing had happened, with the ut-

most formal distinctness, and that it continued to happen, in his mind, he supposed, though he did not know exactly what that meant, and though it seemed to be outside him, before him, about him, and so on. . . .

This may appear as a distinctly obsessive and oblique examination of the nature of experience, but there is no doubting its philosophical penetration. Such passages do not make for easy reading, and indeed there are times when it is almost impossible to continue without one's mind drifting into something akin to involuntary schizophrenia. Yet there is no denying the depth of the philosophical insights achieved in such passages. No other writer had entered into such territory in quite such a manner before. This is the opposite of the Joycean manner which had previously so swamped Beckett. Instead of vast proliferations of meaning there is instead a stripping away of experience to a basic bedrock of meaning. *Watt* may have appeared like a form of madness, just as Beckett himself may have been on the verge of complete breakdown, but he knew what he was doing. This was no inadvertent expression of human extremity and futility, it was instead a conscious investigation of the futility of the human condition in its most fundamental aspects. What it expressed was precisely how Beckett felt at the time; and mirroring such mental disintegration proved a feat of existential revelation.

Watt occupies the hinterland where art shades into philosophy. The practice of one becomes the practice of the other. The deeper resonances are left for us to ponder. The surface ones are more easily discernible. There are evident indications that Mr. Knott is intended as a negation (not; unravelably knotted), a negative version of God. Watt undergoes his quotidian and endlessly repetitive fate, at first with extreme attention and later with some vexation, "And the results, on the whole, were meager." He poses a question (what?) by his very existence—though it is worth noting here that he is not called "Why." His function is epistemological rather than causal. He examines and questions the world in which he finds himself. But, despite the obvious symbolic references in these names,

Beckett insists at the end, "No symbols where none intended." We are given the pointers, the rest we are left free to ponder upon, work out for ourselves, or simply ignore, depending upon our temperament—much as in life. In this way *Watt* may be viewed as anything from a trite comedy to an inscrutable farce (though the profundity of one's reaction should by no means be taken as a reflection of character).

In August 1944, Roussillon was liberated by American troops, but it was a full eight months before Beckett and Suzanne managed to get back to Paris. They discovered much to their relief that the flat in Rue des Favourites had not been ransacked in their absence, a fate that had befallen many other such abandoned properties.

From here Beckett set out for Ireland. Passing through London, he called in at his publishers to discover that *Murphy* had long since been forgotten, and the accumulated royalties he had been hoping to collect were nonexistent. He handed over the manuscript of *Watt*.

On his return to Dublin, Beckett found that his mother had aged considerably in the six years since he had last seen her. The tall proud woman he had known, and fought, was now a bowed old lady who looked all of her seventy-four years. Beckett, for his part, looked emaciated, his face gaunt with suffering. His teeth were in a rotten state, and he was suffering once more from his perennial boils. Much of his time was spent visiting the dentist and consulting the family doctor. In the midst of this, a letter arrived from his publisher, in which the editor gave his reaction to *Watt*, expressing his "very mixed feelings about it and considerable bewilderment. To be quite frank, it is too wild and unintelligible for the most part to stand any chance of successful publication over here at the present time." True originality is seldom acceptable, but its rejection only added further to Beckett's gloom.

Then a further blow struck. To his consternation, Beckett now found his way back to Paris blocked by postwar travel restrictions. After desperate enquiries, he managed to find a position as an interpreter for the Irish Red Cross, which was sending a mission to set up a hospital at St Lô in Normandy. Beckett arrived to find that the town had been reduced to rubble during the D-day landings a year previously, and nothing had changed since. As ever, Beckett responded to the real suffering he encountered here with genuine dedication. When his tour of duty was over, he returned to Paris.

He was now coming up to forty years old, with failure staring him in the face. He had no idea what to do. Since writing was the only thing he *could* do, he began scribbling a few disconnected pieces. By way of a change, he tried writing them in French. Then the money ran out, and he was forced to return to Dublin. Postwar currency restrictions meant that his small private income could not be sent abroad. Once back in Dublin, to the consternation of his mother and brother, he began drinking heavily again, wandering the night streets in a state of profound despair.

It was on one of these nights that he found himself standing on the end of the stone pier at Dun Laoghaire harbor, where he experienced his revelation amidst the howling of the wind and the breaking of the waves, realizing the folly of all that he had previously attempted: "I became aware of my stupidity." All the while he had striven to be knowing, to impart knowledge of one kind or another. His early writings had been swamped by this intellectual knowingness, yet even his later writings had attempted to come to terms with the world, imparting some philosophical apprehension of it. But this had been his big mistake. Instead of trying to write about the outer world, he should have been concentrating on what he *really* felt. He should have been concentrating on what he alone knew, his own feelings, the darkness of his inner world, filled with the uncertainty and hopelessness that constantly dogged him. It was not knowledge he should have been striving to impart, but ignorance. This was his true material, what he had been ignoring all along—the darkness of his own mind.

Realizing this and achieving it were not the same thing. Beckett returned to Paris and began trying to put into practice what he had fleetingly understood. He found that writing in French gave him a certain freedom, allowing him to shed all the intellectual fluency that came so easily to him in English. Here he found a basic style, a simple syntax and unadorned language, which utterly suited his purpose. But how to use this language? He started into a novel about two knockabout Irish characters called Mercier and Camier (Huguenot names, like his own). He described their inept blundering from inconsequential disaster to drunken farce, with much hilarious deadpan dialogue in between. Here was the hoplessness he had been looking for—but still something was not quite right.

There now began the period of Beckett's life which he referred to a "the siege in the room." This would last from 1946 until 1948, during which he would produce his finest work. It was spent largely in his room, isolated from the world, coming face to face with his own demons, attempting to explore the workings of his mind. His routine was for the most part simple enough. He would rise around the early hours of the afternoon, make himself scrambled eggs, and retire to his room for as many hours as he could bear. He would then leave for his late-night perambulation of the bars of Montparnasse, drinking

copious amounts of cheap red wine, returning
before dawn and the long attempt to sleep. His
entire life revolved around his almost psychotic
obsession to write. The writing itself was psychologically painful in the extreme, and to begin
with did not go according to plan. In despair he
attempted to write a long, complex three-act
play called *Eleutheria*, the Greek for freedom.
The play recounted the attempts of a young man
called Viktor Krap to break free from his middle-
class family. The hero's name was indicative of
Beckett's self-esteem during this period. The action of the play took place on a stage divided
into a bourgeois living room and Viktor's bare
room, and involved a variety of characters with
names such as Skunk, Piouk (puke), and Meck
(*mec* is French for pimp). But this proved no
good, and he set it aside. (Though he didn't realize it at the time, both the names and the embry-
onic characters to which they were attached
would continue to grow in his mind, reappearing
years later in all their mature idiosyncracy.) Next
he tried a number of long short stories, and in
the course of these he discovered the solution to

his problem. To reach the truth of his inner experience, he needed to write in monologue. He started into a novel:

> I am in my mother's room. It's I who live there now. I don't know how I got there. Perhaps in an ambulance, certainly a vehicle of some kind. I was helped. I'd never have got there alone. There's this man who comes every week. Perhaps I got here thanks to him. He says not. . . .

Beckett had found his tone of voice and his situation: a bereft character, in isolation, left to the ramblings of his mind. Here was the human condition at its most fundamental.

Beckett had in fact already come very close to this in *Watt*, where he had been aware philosophically of what he was trying to achieve but had allowed the literary element to elude his grasp. The voice had not been there. But now that he had it, he refused to let go of it. Here was the freedom to wander and explore the oddities and absurdities of the human mind, the ebb and flow of thought, the sudden diversions of verbal consciousness. Here Molloy reflects on seeing a nameless character he seems to have known:

> . . . all that inner space one never sees, the brain and heart and other caverns where thought and feeling dance their sabbath. . . . He looks old and it is a sorry sight to see him solitary after so many years, so many days and nights unthinkingly given to that rumor rising at birth and even earlier, What shall I do? What shall I do?, now low, a murmur, now precise as the headwaiter's And to follow? and often rising to a scream. And in the end, or almost, to be abroad alone, by unknown ways, in the gathering night, with a stick.

Such prose may be difficult to follow but often gives up its meaning on a second reading if one ponders the context and jumps of Molloy's thought processes, such as they are. The voice has its own momentum, following the breathing of the narrator. In this voice Beckett had found the freedom to include meditation, poetry, philosophical musings, all filtered through the wry, hard-bitten humor of his own vision. There was no plot, only the occasional rambling story, or memory. The reader, like the writer, was expected to immerse himself in the meandering voice of consciousness. This was not easy, but once achieved was immensely rewarding—by turns entertaining, hilarious, insightful. In this apparent absence of life, all human life was there.

Unexpectedly, in the second half of the book Beckett reverts to the voice of a more recognizably orthodox consciousness. This is Moran, who impinges on the tale of Molloy from his own "objective" viewpoint. Moran is all that Molloy is not, though in many ways they are the opposite sides of the same coin. Between them, they may be said to complete the circle of humanity. Unlike Molloy, Moran believes in willpower, action, and reason. He is a fanatic of habit, a domestic tyrant, obsessed with control. In place of the anarchy of Molloy's mind, we encounter paranoia, sadism, and fixation. Both Molloy and Moran are deranged, but in their own separate ways. To revert to Freudian terms, Molloy is sinking into his unconscious while

Moran is drawn toward his superego. Moran's mission is to find Molloy. His voice is a hilarious parody of ordered consciousness:

> Should I set out on my autocycle? This was the question with which I began. I had a methodical mind and never set out on a mission without prolonged reflection as to the best way of setting out. It was the first problem to solve, at the outset of each enquiry, and I never moved until I had solved it to my satisfaction. Sometimes I took my autocycle, sometimes the train, sometimes the motorcoach, just as sometimes too I left on foot, or on my bicycle, silently, in the night.

When Beckett completed *Molloy*, he realized that his project somehow remained incomplete. He had farther to go, more to say. The second novel, in what would eventually become a trilogy, was called *Malone Dies*. This follows on from the previous two voices (especially Molloy's), taking another step into the darkness of the mind. The central character, Malone, is further removed from everyday reality, a fact that is apparent from the novel's opening words: "I shall soon be quite dead at last in spite of all. Perhaps next month." Malone is an aged, impotent, bedridden figure, on the point of death, and longing for death, but on his own terms, as far as this is possible. The voice of the novel is a voice approaching its own death. What matters now? It is by turns tragic, by turns hilarious, as Malone contemplates his own impotent ending:

> I could die today, if I wished, merely by making a little effort. But it is just as well to let myself die, quietly, without rushing things. Something must have changed. I will not weigh upon the balance any more, one way or the other. I shall be neutral and inert. No difficulty there. Throes are the only trouble. I must be on guard against throes. But I am less given to them now, since coming here. Of course I still have my little fits of impatience, from time to time. . . .

Malone has largely lost interest in his past, and instead of remembering (like Molloy), he passes his time and overcomes his boredom by occasionally inventing stories. Typical of these is the pitiful pointless tale of Lambert and his family who live in misery on their squalid farm "in a hollow, flooded in winter and in summer burnt to a cinder. The way to it leads through a fine meadow. But this fine meadow did not belong to the Lamberts." The only joy in life for Lambert is slaughtering pigs, which he does on an itinerant basis. Another tale is the grotesque love affair between Hairy Mac and Sucky Moll. This even inspires Malone to poetry:

> To the lifelong promised land
> Of the nearest cemetery
> With his Sucky hand in hand
> Love it is at last leads Hairy.

Malone is inspired to ponder on the aged, impotent, and incompetent Hairy Mac:

> And one can only speculate on what he might have achieved if he had become acquainted with true sexuality at a less advanced age.
> I am lost. Not a word.

The novel ends with Malone's voice in mid-story stuttering into the final inarticulate murmurings and silence of death:

> or light light I mean
> never there he will never
> never anything
> there
> any more

The final novel of the trilogy is *The Unnamable*. There is no denying that this is the most difficult of all to read; indeed, one unkind critic christened it "The Unreadable." In keeping with the gradual denuding of humanity that afflicts the voices in Beckett's trilogy, the voice of the Unnamable (who may be called Mahood) is that of someone who appears to exist in a limbo after death and before the full extinction of consciousness. Here Beckett takes his philosophical quest to discover what it is that we are, and how to justify this state to ourselves, to its ultimate conclusion. In *Finnegans Wake*, Joyce had split the atom of the word, releasing a vast energy of allusion.

Beckett set about dealing with the remnants. By this stage, language itself had fallen apart.

> Where now? Who now? When now? Unquestioning. I, say I. Unbelieving. Questions, hypotheses, call them that. Keep going, going on, call that going, call that on. Can it be that one day, off it goes on, that one day I simply stayed in, in where, instead of going out, in the old way, out to spend day and night as far away as possible, it wasn't far. Perhaps that is how it began.

Thus begins one of the most sustained assaults on the foundations of our existential awareness ever written. This opening passage of *The Unnamable* is arguably among the finest philosophical explorations of the twentieth century. Much as the voice of the Unnamable hovers between existence and nonexistence, this passage may be understood as hovering between philosophy and literature. It is neither one nor the other. Too unaesthetic and fragmented to be literature. Too personal (even in this reduced state) to be philosophy. Yet Beckett is telling us that this is the state to which all of philosophy, all literature, can be reduced. This is the earth out of which these separate specializations have flowered. From such fragmented essentials we build the entire edifice of human thought and expression. Founded on such quicksands rests the structure of all our humanity.

As in the previous two novels of the trilogy, the voice mentions previous characters in Beckett's oeuvre. But here it is not simply to refer to them—as if to some past point of navigation on the journey—but to dismiss them:

> All these Murphys, Molloys, and Malones do not fool me. They have made me waste my time, suffer for nothing, speak of them when, in order to stop speaking, I should have spoken of me and of me alone.

These previous attempts have been mere evasions of what it means to be himself. They have been voices smothering the voice which "should have spoken of me." Yet the implication remains that this final unexpressed voice is, ultimately, silence. The voice of the Unnamable is also, it would appear, an evasion. Even so, this voice reaches further toward that inexpressible voice than any before it.

> . . . how can I know, I can't know, if I've spoken of him, I can only speak of me, no, I can't speak of anything, and yet I speak, perhaps it's of him, I'll never know, how could I know, who could know. . . .

And on it goes, in one long unbroken flow of words, for more than one hundred paragraphless pages. This is Beckett's greatest achievement. Yet there is no denying its utter barrenness as art. This is arid territory in the extreme. It may have been necessary for Beckett to cross this territory, "call this going, call this on," but is it necessary for us, the put-upon readers? Do we have to endure all this? If we wish to partake in Beckett's profound divinations, the answer is yes. But many tend to agree with A. A. Alvarez, one of Beckett's most penetrating critics, who declared:

> *The Unnamable* appears flaccid and redundant. It seems to me a classic case of a work

which is necessary but not sufficient; that is to say, personally necessary to Beckett in his exploration of his own limitless negation, but artistically insufficient because of its length, repetitiveness, and private claustrophobia.

Beckett delighted in such philosophical distinctions between necessary and sufficient reason, which hark back to rationalist philosophers such as Descartes and Leibniz. If Beckett's trilogy is seen as an extended examination of Descartes' famous *Cogito ergo sum* (I think therefore I am), then *The Unnamable* is undoubtedly as close a scrutiny of the qualities inherent in *sum* (being) as one is likely to find. But any answer to set against Alvarez's objection must confront the question: Is the experience evoked in *The Unnamable* purely subjective, or does it have universal resonance? The answer here would appear to be that such depictions belong to Beckett's crisis-ridden psychology. Most, if not all of us, do not spend our time as nameless beings in a limbo on the verge of nonexistence. Yet by the same count most of us never see a starry night as depicted by Van Gogh.

The psychological disintegration is in the end irrelevant to the work (whether it be art, literature, philosophy, or quasi-religious experience). Entering into the world of *The Unnamable* we are led to a heightened philosophical awareness of our existence. This may appear to be no wondrous experience, as it is when we enter into the vision of Van Gogh's starry night. The operative word here is "appear," for Beckett's *The Unnamable* is indeed a wondrous world, filled with insight into what, at its most reduced, is the nature of our condition. As Plato said, "Philosophy begins in wonder." *The Unnamable* is also a work of wonder, in its own way as wondrous as Van Gogh's so very different vision. Where Van Gogh visualizes, Beckett wonders. He wonders in all senses of the word: he questions, and he marvels. Just because his latter awareness is filled with a sense of the absurdity of existence does not in any way reduce its power.

So they build up hypotheses which collapse on top of one another, it's human, a lobster couldn't do it. Ah a nice mess we're in, the

58

whole pack of us, is it possible we're all in the same boat, no, we're in a nice mess each in his own peculiar way. I myself have been scandalously bungled, they must be beginning to realize it. . . .

Until the voice of the Unnamable finally fades away, amidst the murmurs, having come to no conclusion other than the fact that there is no conclusion, in any sense, except ultimate silence:

> . . . it will be I, it will be the silence, where I am, I don't know, I'll never know, in the silence you don't know, you must go on, I can't go on, I'll go on.

Surprising though it may seem, Beckett's precision, at this final point and others in *The Unnamable*, leaves much open to the reader. These are the final words, the ultimate gasp, of consciousness. Read them as a slow, finally diminishing, murmurous gasping, as they fade before death, and they become an acquiescence to the silence, to nothingness. Read them as the last desperate ravening attempt of the voice to finally

grasp itself and arrive at some form of understanding, and they become altogether something
else. They may contain all the human fear of
death, they may become a final defiance, a gesture against inevitable oblivion, even a final absurdity, or an ultimate agony. It might be difficult
to read *The Unnamable* in more than limited
doses, but it is open to the acclimatization of any
mind. Each passage can be the gnomic prose-
poem of our own experience.

Beckett worked in pared-down language, a
reductionist vocabulary that he made very much
his own. He insisted upon extreme control of his
words, his phrases, even to the extent of control-
ling how we breathe them, how we absorb them.
There is an onward flow, made up of phrased
breaths, lulling us into the rhythm of his voice,
his thoughts. But curiously it is this very control
of his words which gives us such a great freedom
in experiencing them. Precision in this one aspect
allows us freedom in many others. A passage
that we may read as tragedy one day, can easily
appear hilarious the next time we read it. Beckett may have been unable to grasp the impossi-

ble, but he knew very well what he was leaving open to the possible. The trilogy consists of monologues, with no director's instructions on how they should be read. We are the directors. We each learn from Beckett in our own way. The voices are enlivened by what each one of us puts into them.

When Beckett had finished the second work of his trilogy, *Malone Dies*, he found himself at loose ends. To take his mind off things before facing up to the psychological rigors of *The Unnamable*, he began writing the play that eventually became *Waiting for Godot*. As Beckett himself put it, he "began to write *Godot* as a relaxation, to get away from the awful prose I was writing at the time." ("Awful" in this context refers to the experience of writing the trilogy rather than making a qualitative judgment on its style. Beckett was certainly aware of what he was achieving; though like any artist moving into new territory, he had to live with the prospect that the critics might indeed dismiss his efforts as awful.)

It was ironic that this "diversion" which Beckett now began writing should eventually prove to be his best-known work. *Waiting for Godot* is at present the most frequently performed twentieth-century play throughout the world. Yet the entire drama centers on two derelict characters who do little other than fritter away their time "waiting for Godot." Accounting for the play's popularity is thus no easy matter. With some justice, this two-act drama has been described as a play where "nothing happens—twice." Others claim that it captures, in essence, the nihilistic philosophy that best characterizes the twentieth century. Still others insist that it expresses a particular state of human mental evolution, one which civilized humanity has evolved to come to terms with the rigors and uncertainties, horrors and transformations that continue to underlie the comforts and apparent certainties of modern life. At the same time there is no denying that had *Waiting for Godot* been staged as a medieval mystery play, its medieval audience would probably have recognized and understood many of its themes. A peasant audience of the era that experienced the Black Death would have empathized with two suffering tramps in a blighted landscape, their endless waiting for the arrival of "Godot," their preoccupation with redemption, and the futility of a world in which "Godot" was absent— to say nothing of their absurd philosophical bickering and the broad, slapstick humor of their situation. *Waiting for Godot* is both archetypically twentieth century and as timeless as its reduced characters in their empty landscape. Humanity of all ages has found itself, at least momentarily, in a world where "Godot" appears to be absent, a world just as impossible to understand as that which Beckett portrays. Here, it would appear, is the ultimate "Much ado about nothing." Yet it surely must be about something.

So what exactly *is Waiting for Godot* about? To put the obvious question in its most blatant form: Is "Godot" God? Are the two main characters, Vladimir and Estragon, waiting for some kind of divine revelation? Beckett always strongly denied that "Godot" was God—one of the few points on which he was uncharacteristically explicit and adamant regarding his work. But the fact remains that "Godot"—at least to

English audiences—does contain the word God. On the other hand, to a German audience it would appear to contain an elision of *Gott* and *Tod* ("God" and "Death": as perhaps in "God is dead"). The latter would appear to be a more likely explanation—for those who require such crass simplicities. Beckett certainly detested this type of narrowing-down of his work, not wishing it to be blighted by literalist interpretations.

We should not search for a key to the inherent enigma. This is precisely what his work is *not* about. The puzzle has no correct answer: the situation cannot be resolved. If answer we need, we should seek it within ourselves—and keep it there. The purpose of the play, if purpose it can be called, is to remind us of the essential situation in which we find ourselves. *Waiting for Godot* is a tragicomedy about atmosphere, situation, and condition, much more than it is about meaning. Its meaning could well be explained as the absence of meaning. Its action is the response of the characters to the futile situation in which they find themselves. This response is both heartrending and hilarious.

Vladimir goes towards Estragon, contemplates him a moment, then shakes him awake.

ESTRAGON: (*wild gestures, incoherent words. Finally*). Why will you never let me sleep?

VLADIMIR: I felt lonely.

ESTRAGON: I was dreaming I was happy.

VLADIMIR: That passed the time.

ESTRAGON: I was dreaming that—

VLADIMIR: (*violently*). Don't tell me!

One must always bear in mind that Beckett wrote *Waiting for Godot* as a *divertissement* from the awe-ful confrontation of his prose. The comedy is often farcical, in the manner of early Chaplin. Elements, especially in the tramplike appearance of Vladimir and Estragon, are purposely Chaplinesque—their actions likewise, with dropping trousers and other ludicrous incidents. At the same time the relationship between these two main characters bears many similarities to that of Laurel and Hardy. They are both fond of each other and exasperated with each other. Despite their differences, they are in their different ways utterly dependent upon each other: they could not survive alone. Their exchanges both goad and encourage. They enable them to pass the time, to avoid facing up to their situation. Their endless conversation contains much affectionate, well-honed repartee. According to Beckett's friends, his wrangling conversations with Suzanne often took on this same conscious Music Hall quality of ritual and repartee. This appears to have first developed during their long trek south through war-torn France, as a means of overcoming the tedium and suffering of their journey.

> VLADIMIR: (*sententious*) To every man his little cross. (*He sighs.*) Till he dies. (*Afterthought.*) And is forgotten.
>
> ESTRAGON: In the meantime let us try and converse calmly, since we are incapable of keeping silent.
>
> VLADIMIR: You're right, we're inexhaustible.
>
> ESTRAGON: It's so we won't think.
>
> VLADIMIR: We have that excuse.

ESTRAGON: It's so we won't hear.
VLADIMIR: We have our reasons.

The scenery, or lack of it ("A country road. A tree.") would seem to depict some featureless rural spot somewhere in France—though it could almost as easily be some barren spot in the Wicklow Mountains, where Beckett had spent so much time on lonely walks, listening to the voices of his own mind, arguing with himself. Vladimir is the tall, thin, intellectual figure who has seen better times. Estragon is short and fat, with occasional female undertones to his character.

VLADIMIR: Do you remember the Gospels?
ESTRAGON: I remember the maps of the Holy Land. Colored they were. Very pretty. The Dead Sea was pale blue. The very look of it made me thirsty. That's where we'll go, I used to say, that's where we'll go for our honeymoon. We'll swim. We'll be happy.
VLADIMIR: You should have been a poet.

ESTRAGON: I was. (*Gesture towards his rags.*)
Isn't that obvious. (*Silence.*)
VLADIMIR: Where was I. . . . How's your foot?
ESTRAGON: Swelling visibly.

Along with the misery, there is of course the tedium. As Estragon puts it, "Nothing happens, nobody comes, nobody goes, it's awful!"

At one point on their blasted heath, however, Vladimir and Estragon encounter another strange couple—Pozzo and Lucky. The self-important Pozzo carries a whip and leads his servant Lucky by a rope around his neck. Lucky is weighed down, carrying his master's various possessions, including a picnic basket and a stool. Pozzo and Lucky appear as a parody of the master-servant relationship. But there are also elements of psychological metaphor here, with Pozzo as the ego, or even commanding superego, and Lucky as the unconscious mind. Before they take their leave, Pozzo makes Lucky give a performance in which he "thinks aloud." Whereupon Lucky simply opens his mouth and delivers a torrent of words, an uninterrupted jumble of nonsense and cliché, continuing in a flow of association:

> LUCKY: . . . Fulham Clapham in a word the dead loss per caput since the death of Bishop Berkeley being to the tune of one inch four ounce per caput approximately by and large more or less to the nearest decimal good measure round figures stark naked in stockinged feet in Connemara. . . .

Pozzo and Lucky proceed on their way but are encountered again in the second act. This time Pozzo is blind and Lucky is dumb. Lucky is still carrying Pozzo's possessions, but he is now leading Pozzo, who follows him by hanging onto the rope around Lucky's neck. Despite this, Pozzo is still very much in charge. Again, their relationship is open to political or psychological interpretation but is best appreciated as the farcical personal situation it purports to be. Here is Laurel and Hardy taken one step further—instead of a loose, knockabout personal relationship, as with Vladimir and Estragon, we now have an inflexible power relationship.

As Pozzo prepares to leave, Estragon asks him, "Where do you go from here?" Pozzo replies simply, "On." Such purposeless endurance is a theme that runs throughout the play. The first act ends:

> *Silence.*
> ESTRAGON: Well, shall we go?
> VLADMIR: Yes, let's go.
> *They do not move.*

The second act finally ends in identical fashion. The bemused, chastened, or entertained audience eventually breaks the ensuing silence with sporadic and then mounting applause—frequently interspersed with cheers, boos, and catcalls. *Waiting for Godot* had a mixed reception from the beginning, and there is something about its challenging informality and apparent formlessness that seems to release an audience from its inhibitions. Few leave the theatre without their own very definite opinions having been provoked. No one wishes to feel that he (or she) has been made a fool of—either in the theatre or in real life. And life, or drama, in Beckettian form can easily be seen as a load of rubbish. Or alternatively, as refreshingly free from comforting preconceptions. Stoic indifference among audiences of Beckett's plays is rare.

When Beckett finally completed both *Waiting for Godot* and his trilogy he lapsed into apathetic exhaustion. The psychological toll involved in the intense introspection of the trilogy had been immense. In the midst of this, his mother fell seriously ill, and it became clear that she had not long to live. Beckett returned to Dublin, where all the guilt and angst he had experienced with regard to his mother surfaced once more as he attended her deathbed, watching her die. After the funeral he returned to Paris, where his constant state of despair was punctuated by nights of drinking. His failure as a human being and as an artist now seemed all but complete. A photograph from this period shows a skeletally thin figure with a bemused, all but defeated, expression. Yet he had done what he had felt impelled to do. The artist in him had fulfilled himself in his own willful way. In his perversity he had undeniably achieved uniqueness.

But the self-lacerating human being in him was aware that what he had produced was all but incomprehensible to anyone else. No one would ever want to read such unreadable prose, let alone put on such undramatic drama.

Although Beckett appeared no longer to believe in himself, one person at least still retained faith in his baffling work. This was Suzanne. She reproached Beckett for not sending out his manuscripts. He merely shrugged, telling her to "do whatever you want with them." So she decided she would do just that. If Beckett wouldn't attempt to have his work published, or performed, she would. Tenaciously she lugged his manuscripts from one small Parisian publisher to another, leaving the manuscript of *Waiting for Godot* at the door of a succession of small avant-garde theatres. It was only through her persistence, in the face of any number of puzzled or dismissive rejections, that Beckett's work ever saw the light of day.

In 1951, Suzanne's efforts finally came to fruition, of a kind. A French editor with a soft spot for Ireland and all things Celtic imagined he had come across a typical example of classic Irish humor, a rarity which was all but unknown in French translation. As a result, *Molloy*, and then *Malone Dies*, were eventually published in French in a limited edition by Editions de Minuit (Midnight Editions), the former clandestine resistance publishers. The appearance of these two difficult novels attracted a few favorable mentions in avant-garde literary magazines, but little widespread recognition or commercial success—causing the publishers to abandon the idea of bringing out *The Unnamable*. Instead they issued the script of *Waiting for Godot*, which appeared in 1952. Some months later the owner of the tiny Théâtre de Babylone on the Left Bank agreed to stage the play. Although neither Beckett nor Suzanne realized it, he had already given up on the theatre. "I am going to close up shop, and I may as well close up on a beauty," he told Beckett's friend Roger Blinn, the avant-garde director who had agreed to see the play through production.

So rehearsals began. Despite Beckett's shyness, he soon began taking an increasingly interfering and dominant role in these sessions. As one of the actors remarked, "Beckett does not want his actors to act. He wants them to do what he tells them. When they try to act, he becomes very angry." Beckett knew precisely what he wanted. "There is nothing more grotesque than tragedy," he explained cryptically. His plays were not intended to be naturalistic, more ritualistic—the parts required an interpretation that was stylized rather than psychological. Yet despite his increasing involvement, he refused to give any hint to the actors of the "meaning" of what was taking place on the stage.

Beckett would always insist upon taking such a leading role in the production of his plays. This can in part be explained by his origins as a novelist, where the medium is simply words, of which the writer remains in complete control. Also, there is no doubt that Beckett's plays did, at least initially, require a certain mannered production in order to achieve their own conviction. After all, audiences had simply never seen anything like this before. Later, however, Beckett's mania for control would have a cramping effect on his dramatic works—and even today his trustees, who

hold the performance rights, retain a severely re-
strictive control over productions of his work.
Beckett's plays will surely take on a new unfore-
seen lease of life when this control is relaxed.

The first performance of *Waiting for Godot*
was staged on January 5, 1953. Beckett stayed
away, unable to face the ordeal of witnessing his
own first night. The audience, seated on 230
folding chairs in a cramped space, was bewildered, but a number of perceptive critics immediately recognized the play's originality and worth.
Beckett was acclaimed as "one of today's best
playwrights," and it was predicted that his play
"would be spoken of for a long time." *Waiting
for Godot* struck a chord with the postwar ni-
hilism of existentialist Paris, where Jean-Paul
Sartre was the philosopher-king and Juliet
Greco's fatalistic songs were all the rage in the
cafés of the Latin Quarter. The audiences at *Waiting for Godot* remained baffled but continued to
fill the tiny theatre night after night. Soon "all
Paris" knew that something special was taking
place at the Théâtre de Babylone. The tide had finally turned, and Beckett was on his way to

75

achieving the recognition of which he had so long secretly dreamt.

Productions of *Waiting for Godot* were soon opening in London (1955), the United States (1956), and then throughout the world. International reactions were remarkably similar. Packed audiences were bewildered, and often the theatres were more than half empty after intermission. But many critics recognized that this was the play that somehow seemed appropriate to our age. The drama of the two tramps who did nothing, twice over, was more than a reflection of fashionable Parisian angst; it touched something in the very soul of modern humanity. Night after night audiences filled the theatres, to be bewildered and boo, or to have their eyes opened and applaud. Controversy rather than acceptance was the initial ingredient that contributed to Beckett's success, and soon *Waiting for Godot* was being performed on avant-garde stages and small theatres from Santiago to Stockholm. In the process of becoming an underground hit, it gradually established itself as a permanent classic of the world's theatre repertoire.

Beckett meanwhile returned to his desk. Following the completion of his trilogy, he produced thirteen brief *Texts for Nothing*, which he referred to as an "afterbirth" of the trilogy. The monologuist prose is similar, as well as being similarly difficult and rewarding, to that of *The Unnamable*. The voice questions its condition, attempting to grasp the ever-elusive truth of its being. The philosophical quest resembles a snake attempting to swallow its own tale: "No voice ever but in my life, it says, if speaking of me one can speak of life, and it can. . . ." As ever, even at his most impenetrable, Beckett's words are seldom devoid of graveyard humor.

> Did I try everything, ferret in every hold, secretly, silently, patiently, listening? I'm in earnest, as so often, I'd like to be sure I left no stone unturned before reporting me missing and giving up.

The attempt remains as ambitious as ever:

> I'm the clerk, I'm the scribe, at the hearings of what cause I know not. Why want it to be mine, I don't want it.

Or:

> Where would I go, if I could go, who would
> I be, if I could be, what would I say, if I had
> a voice, who says this, saying it's me?

After these *Texts*, Beckett returned once more
to the theatre, eventually producing his second
major drama, *Endgame*. This features the dying
Hamm in black glasses confined to his wheel-
chair. He is attended by his servant, the recalci-
trant Clov; also present are Hamm's mother and
father, Nagg and Nell, who inhabit dustbins,
having apparently lost their legs many years previously in a bicycle accident. The characters'
roles are indicated by their names: Hamm (ham-
mer), Clov (*clou* is French for nail), Nagg (*Nagel*
is German for nail), and Nell (Irish accent, nail).
There are of course many other allusions: Hamm
(as in ham actor), Nagg (to nag), even Nell (as in
the tolling of the death knell). All the action
takes place in a claustrophobic spherical structure with two high windows, resembling the inside of a skull. The outside of the skull appears
to be a landscape after a nuclear holocaust. Thus

the characters may also be seen as the elements of a mind as it faces death and final extinction. So far so bad.

The title *Endgame* refers to the last moves in a chess game, with Hamm as the king desperately trying to avoid the checkmate of death. This is all very unrelentingly grim, and although the play certainly has its humorous moments, the atmosphere remains persistently oppressive, not to say depressive. Unlike *Waiting for Godot*, there is no looseness—either of action or inaction, resonance or repartee. The author is more in control, and yet the words have none of the bleak memorableness of *Godot*. This said, the play is not without its moments:

CLOV: (*despairingly*). Ah . . . !
HAMM: Something. . . . From your heart.
CLOV: My heart!
HAMM: A few words. . . . From your heart.
Pause.
CLOV: (*Fixed gaze, tonelessly, towards auditorium*) They said to me, That's love, yes yes, no doubt, now you see how—

HAMM: Articulate!

CLOV: (*as before*). How easy it is. They said to me, That's friendship, yes yes, no question. You've found it. They said to me, Here's the place, stop, raise your head and look at all that beauty. That order! They said to me, Come now, you're not a brute beast, think upon these things and you'll see how all becomes clear. And simple! They said to me, What skilled attention they get, all these dying of their wounds.

HAMM: Enough!

The unremitting bleakness of *Endgame* was not so well received, but it is now generally regarded as a masterpiece of its kind—second, though a long way second, to *Waiting for Godot*.

As if to show that he was not entirely lost in depression, Beckett now turned to another *divertissement*, a brief dramatic work entitled *Krapp's Last Tape*. This was written in English, and Beckett's easy familiarity with his mother tongue enabled his imagination to take wing. *Krapp's Last Tape* is too short to be considered a major masterpiece (the entire script, including copious stage directions, covers just nine pages), but in other aspects it may well be compared to *Waiting for Godot*. It is also the most accessible and most obviously personal (in the literal, realistic sense) of his later works. The central and only appearing character is Krapp, an echo of the name given by Beckett to the autobiographical character in his earlier failed play *Eleutheria*. But here Krapp takes on a life of his own. No longer derisively autobiographical, he becomes intensely so, and in doing so transcends his particularities to become one of the great archetypical characters of the modern stage. He is by turns funny, pathetic, farcical, and deeply touching— all in the space of such a brief stage life!

The curtain goes up to reveal Krapp in his sparse and decrepit den. He is an old man, playing over and again the tapes that he has recorded during his life. These tapes are a form of journal, in which he describes what has happened to him and also summarizes his current attitude to life. We hear his resolutions, his criticisms of his former self, his regrets. We witness the older Krapp listening to the younger man recounting his most poignant memories—the death of his mother, his love, his great moment of inspiration.

These minutes on stage imply volumes, evoking an entire life as well as the feeling of its unfulfillment and irretrievability. The older Krapp and the younger Krapp both speak. They are two different people—the one unheard by the other, the one a stranger to the other. We hear their separate voices, but there is no dialogue—they can never speak to each other, the past can never be repaired. Krapp, playing and rewinding the spools of his ancient recording machine, meditatively munching on his bananas, occasionally disappearing into the darkness for a swig of hootch, is one of the most moving figures of the modern stage, despite his brief stage life, which remains in the mind long after it is witnessed. At the end we leave the aged Krapp with his "sour cud and iron stool," listening bitterly to the callow judgment and hope of his younger voice on the tape:

TAPE: . . . Perhaps my best years are gone. When there was a chance of happiness. But

I wouldn't want them back. Not with the fire in me now. No, I wouldn't want them back.

[KRAPP *motionless staring before him. The tape runs on in silence.*]

CURTAIN

In 1960, Beckett began another novel, which was eventually called *Comment C'est*. In English this is translated as *How It Is*, which loses the resonances of the French title—*commencer* (to begin) and *comme on sait* (how one knows). Here Beckett faced an apparently insurmountable problem: How was he to progress beyond the apparent dead end of *The Unnamable*? How was he to go any further than that expiring monologue without going back on himself? How was he to create a novel when he had to all intents and purposes killed off this genre to his own satisfaction?

Taking a cue from his plays, Beckett gave the central voice a setting—though in keeping with his plays, this was bleak in the extreme. The initially unnamed narrator is crawling through a sea of mud, in the course of which he encounters various similar figures. Behind them they all drag their few miserable possessions, tied up in sacks. During the second part of the novel the narrator encounters Pim, in the course of which he reveals that his own name is Bom. This encounter is a grotesque parody of human intercourse (in all senses) as the two figures grapple and entwine in the mud, before going on their separate ways. Bom characterizes himself as "hanging on by the fingernails to one's condition," and this is certainly no exaggeration. During the course of his progress through the mud he has occasional vivid memories of a more realistic life. Some of these are distinctly autobiographical, though the suicide of Bom's wife appears to be a mélange of quasi-autobiographical guilt and wish-fulfillment. (Things were not going well with Suzanne.)

This novel, if such it can be called, consists entirely of brief unpunctuated paragraphs, which appear to incorporate their own breathlike rhythm, if not meaning:

This voice these voices no knowing not
meaning a choir no no only one but quaqua
meaning on all sides megaphones possible
technique something wrong here

Wrong for never twice the same unless time
vast tracts aged out of recognition no for often fresher stronger after than before unless
sickness sorrow they sometimes pass one
feels better less wretched after than before

Unlike the similarly unreadable *Unnamable*,
How It Is has meager rewards for those who per-
sist with the narrator across this mired literary
bogland.

From it I learn from it I learned what little remained learn what little remains of how it
was before Pim with Pim after Pim and how
it is for that too it found words.

And so on, for pages on end, without relief. The
critics were baffled, and even some of Beckett's
most dedicated aficionados confessed themselves

at a loss. In destroying the novel, this time Beckett appeared to have destroyed his own writing.

By now Beckett's life with Suzanne had descended into a characteristic farce. His general behavior and attitude toward the world, to say nothing of his heavy drinking and occasional affairs, made him impossible to live with. (After all, he too found it all but impossible to live with himself.) He and Suzanne still shared an apartment but had come to a unique arrangement. Inside the front door, the apartment had two doors—one leading to his separate quarters, the other leading to hers. When Beckett wanted to communicate with Suzanne, he called her on the telephone. Despite this apparent alienation, their bond remained deep. They shared too much ever to part fully. Beckett never forgot all that Suzanne had done for him—the tireless efforts she had made to unload his manuscripts on uninterested readers. She was also the one who had lived with him, and stood by him, during his times of greatest travail. She alone had witnessed and shared his deepest miseries. In 1961, Beckett decided to marry Suzanne—as a show of good faith, as a recognition of what she had done, and to ensure that if he died she would inherit the considerable fortune that was accumulating from the worldwide royalties earned by his works. Typically they traveled in secret to England, where they were married without fuss or friends in the anonymous coastal town of Folkestone. Beckett's only indication of where he was or what he was doing was a typically oblique postcard to a friend in Paris: "Blood flows more calmly in the town of Harvey." (William Harvey, who discovered the circulation of the blood, was born in Folkestone in 1578.)

From now on Beckett increasingly busied himself with translations of his own work, from French into English, as well as "overseeing" productions of his own plays in English, French, and German (in which he was also fluent). In between he wrote a number of more or less successful "dramaticules" and short prose pieces. Among these was a brief film script entitled simply *Film*. This was to star the great silent movie actor Buster Keaton, whose expressionless "stone face" had become his nickname and stock-in-trade. Beckett was a great admirer of Keaton and in 1964 traveled to New York to assist in the production of *Film*. The aging Keaton agreed to emerge from his full-time poker-playing retirement only because he needed the money. His initial reaction was to declare that the apparently simple but philosophically profound script was quite beyond him. After a few contretemps, he moodily went through the motions in front of the camera, with no attempt to act. Beckett was delighted, this was precisely what he required. Alas, offscreen Keaton continued simply to go through the motions, and there was no meeting of minds between these two great "stone faces" of the twentieth century.

Beckett's shorter prose pieces are another acquired taste. They are by turn elusive and allusive. Despite such difficulty, they are well worth the effort. Readers will discover their own favorites among these more or less impenetrable texts. One of the more successful is the 1963 piece *Imagination Dead Imagine*, in which the central voice attempts to do just that, coming to the realization: "No, life ends and no, there is nothing elsewhere, and no question now of ever finding again that white speck lost in whiteness. . . ."

In October 1969, Beckett learned that he had won the Nobel Prize for Literature. At the time he was holidaying at a remote coastal resort in Tunisia. To his horror, the world's press descended upon his hotel, and he was besieged in his room. The pathologically shy and retiring Beckett was eventually persuaded to present himself to the press, where he faced a barrage of cameras. He was too overcome to reply to their questions and simply sat there with his head bowed, as if in shame. His health, frail at the best of times, took some time to recover from the shock.

On his return to Paris, Beckett took up his translations again, occasionally producing another short prose piece or dramaticule. These latter are for the most part boldly experimental. For instance, *Breath* consists of just a page of instructions. Its setting is an empty stage, littered with rubbish: "No verticals, all scattered and lying." The action, such as it is, consists of a cry, later repeated, and the amplified recording of a deep breath, which inhales and then exhales ("inspiration . . . expiration," in the words of the stage directions) while a dim light slowly increases and then decreases. The entire "drama" takes less than a minute. Yet, in the right circumstances, it can produce a striking effect, giving pause for thought. Our breath is our very life, our inspiration and our expiration. What could be more simple? This, basically, is all we are.

Some of these dramaticules work, others are strangely unsatisfactory—being both slight and profound at the same time. But even in this form Beckett was able to produce the occasional masterpiece. One among these is *Not I*. It is, again, reductionist in the extreme. The stage is in darkness, with a spotlight focused on a mouth, which speaks through a hole in the black backcloth. Downstage is a dark listening figure. The female mouth speaks in a torrent of disjointed, all but meaningless words. Gradually the effect of the naked isolated mouth and its jumble of words and phrases takes on a mesmerizing and powerful meaning of its own.

... so disconnected ... never got the message
... or powerless to respond ... like numbed
... couldn't make the sound ... not any
sound ... no sound of any kind ... no
screaming for help for example ... should
she feel so inclined ... scream ... [*Screams.*]
... then listen ... [*Silence.*] ... scream again
... [*Screams again.*] ... then listen again ...
[*Silence.*] ... no ... spared that ...

The effect is both horrific and tragic, and appears to express the being of humanity on a
deeply fundamental level. It is primitive, inarticulate, yet seems to be groping toward some extreme of articulacy.

... no idea ... what she was saying ... imagine! ... no idea what she was saying! ... till
she began trying to ... delude herself ...
it was not hers at all ... not her voice at all
... and no doubt would have ... vital she
should ...

After fifteen minutes of this the audience is aware
that it is undergoing a profound and primal

experience. The precise nature of the experience remains elusive, causing us to ponder on it long after the event. In some performances *Not I* is repeated after an interval. Curiously, this does not always work. The piece is best seen (and heard), on its own, and then left at that. The sight of that almost obscene, isolated mouth, giving voice to the words, takes on a chthonic life of it own.

> . . . now can't stop . . . imagine! . . . can't stop the stream . . . and the whole brain begging . . . something begging in the brain . . . begging the mouth to stop . . .

This is the stream, the scream, the unstoppable, unbearable torrent of consciousness, the unending, unstoppable voice in the head that goes on regardles of sense, of meaning, of suffering. How our life is comprised of this unending gossip which goes on and on in our brain. . . . Yet in a way, ultimately this is all we have.

The short prose pieces that Beckett continued to write were for the most part less successful. But they too contained occasional flashes of genius, such as could not have been produced by anyone else. Beckett was determined to go on, no matter what—as he put it encouragingly: "fail again, fail better." Among the more successful of these pieces are *Lessness*, *Enough*, and *Old Earth*, the last of which begins with the memorable: "Old earth, no more lies. . . ."

These pieces attempt to reach the very heart of the human experience, to grasp our essential being, to gain inklings into what, ultimately, experience is. This is literature so close to philosophy as to be indistinguishable. It is a form of creative philosophy, and as such harks back to Descartes' "I think, therefore I am." One of Descartes' best-known works is his *Meditations*, and this is precisely what he was doing when he was philosophizing—meditating upon what he called the first, or ultimate, philosophy. These later pieces of Beckett's short prose may also be seen as meditations on the process of living and thinking, attempts to come to terms with, and understand, the full import of Descartes' famous conclusion. Beckett's meditations include both more and less of our humanity than Descartes'. They discard the rational calm of Descartes, the civilized vision of the Enlightenment. Beckett's voices, his beings, express all our irrational fears yet always retain an element of their rationality. Even when reason is lost, it is eventually regained, so that its absence can be rationally assessed and the endurance can continue. The endurance itself ("I must go on") is a persistence far deeper than rationality; it is the persistence of life itself. This is how our being evolved, this is how we emerged from the primeval slime to become what we are.

Beckett's vision remains open to all manner of irrationality. "We are all born mad, some remain so." Yet at the same time it is focused by its reductionism. "They give birth astride a grave, the light gleams an instant, then it's night once more." Beckett concentrates upon that gleaming instant like no other.

In his late seventies, Beckett's years of ill health and heavy drinking began to tell. In 1986 he became prey to recurrent bouts of giddiness, which caused him to have several serious falls, both at home and in the street. By now Suzanne was in her mid-eighties and ailing too. Age had caused a deterioration in her normally stoic character; as a result she suffered from bouts of anger, much of which she directed at Beckett. For his part, Beckett was deeply upset by this turn of events.

In 1987 he moved into an old people's home. This was a modest establishment, and Beckett lived in a sparse room, with just a few books and his bottle of Irish whiskey in the cupboard. Outside was a bleak garden with a single Godot-like tree. Friends who called were shocked at Beckett's impoverished quarters, but he refused to spend his considerable fortune on anything better. He had all that he needed. In July 1989, Suzanne died, and the eighty-three-year-old Beckett followed her five months later, December 22, 1989.

Afterword

To add an afterword, after such ultimate words as Beckett's, would seem more than presumptuous. Still, it is worth briefly considering the after-*life* of his words. Beckett's works continue to divide their readers and audiences, and the feelings evoked are seldom less than impassionate. "Sam" is either a great personal favorite, subject to much hero worship, or "Beckett" is reviled as a load of pretentious nonsense, as filled with rubbish as the stages of his plays.

In the eyes of his admirers, Beckett has attained the canon of "great literature." Such status is extremely difficult to achieve—but once achieved is all but impossible to lose. It is doubtful that Beckett's detractors, even the most learned, commonsensical, or prestigious, will succeed in dethroning him while each new generation of young readers finds such rapport with his works. Pessimism such as Beckett's always has its appeal. It mocks experience, authority, and achievement: all that stand in the way of the young. Yet the appeal of Beckett's perversely determined brand of pessimism is not limited to the young. It has an ability to withstand the slings and arrows of outrageous fortune—to which youth may be particularly prone, but which in old age become a permanent condition. The philosophy of such pessimism bursts the rainbow soap bubbles of illusion, leaving us blinking with stinging eyes at unremitting reality. Yet such defeatism is no soft option. Beckett had iron in his soul: his was the wry humor of those with fortitude, those who withstand all misfortune. His voices may be those of the defeated, of the truly hopeless in their various guises, but the fact is that they never admitted final defeat. ". . . In the silence you don't know, you must go on, I can't go on, I'll go on."

Beckett's Chief Works
in English

Beckett translated almost all of his own later works from French into English. These translations are often slightly different from the originals, and unlike so many translations are literary works in their own right, quite the equal of their originals.

Whoroscope (1930)†
More Pricks Than Kicks (1934)†
Echo's Bones and Other Precipitates (1935)†
Murphy (1938)*†

*denotes major works
†discussed in text

Waiting for Godot (1953)*†
Watt (1953)*†
Molloy (1955)*†
Malone Dies (1956)*†
The Unnamable (1958)*†
Endgame (1958)*†
Krapp's Last Tape (1958)*†
Embers (1959)
How It Is (1964)†
Film (1964)†
Imagination Dead Imagine (1965)†
Texts for Nothing (1967)*†
Breath (1969)†
Not I (1972)*†
Mercier and Camier (1974)†
Old Earth (1974)†
All That Fall (1979)

Chronology of Beckett's Life and Times

1906	Samuel Beckett born on Good Friday, April 13, second son of William and May Beckett, at Foxrock, south Dublin, Ireland.
1914–1918	World War I.
1916	Easter Rising in Dublin by Irish patriots against British rule.
1922	Ireland gains independence from Britain, with Ulster (Northern Ireland) remaining British.
1922–1923	Irish civil war.

1920–1923	Beckett becomes boarder at Portora Royal School in Ulster.
1923–1927	Studies modern languages (English, French, Italian) at Trinity College, Dublin.
1927	Wins gold medal for best scholar in final exams.
1927–1928	Beckett teaches for two terms at Campbell College, Belfast.
1928	Goes to Paris as Reader at École Normale Supérieure. Meets James Joyce.
1929	Wall Street crash signals worldwide Great Depression. Beckett's first publication, essay "Dante . . . Bruno. Vico . . . Joyce."
1930	Beckett's poem *Whoroscope* wins Cunard Prize in Paris.
1930–1932	Becomes lecturer in French at Trinity College, Dublin. Resigns after four terms.
1931	Publishes *Proust* in London.

1932   Beginning of Beckett's five years of wandering in Germany, France, England, and Ireland.

1933   Hitler comes to power in Germany. Beckett's father dies, leaving him small private income. Begins two-year stay in Chelsea, London.

1934   Beckett undergoes period of psychoanalysis. Publishes collection of short stories, *More Pricks Than Kicks*, in London.

1935   Breaks off psychoanalysis. Publishes collection of poems, *Echo's Bones and Other Precipitates*, in Paris.

1937   Settles permanently in Paris.

1938   Seriously wounded in stabbing incident in Montmartre. Lives together with Suzanne Deschevaux-Dumesnil. First novel, *Murphy*, published in London.

1939   Outbreak of World War II, in which Ireland remains neutral.

1940	German invasion and occupation of France. Beckett registers as neutral national living in Paris.
1941	Joins cell of underground French Resistance.
1942	Resistance cell in which Beckett is involved penetrated by Germans. Beckett and Suzanne flee Paris for South of France; eventually settle at Roussillon in unoccupied Vichy France. Beckett supports himself as farm laborer and begins writing *Watt*.
1944	Paris liberated by Allied troops. Beckett and Suzanne return to Paris.
1945	End of World War II. Beckett returns to Ireland, finishes writing *Watt*. Returns to France, working for Irish Red Cross in Normandy. Awarded Croix de Guerre for his work in French Resistance. Begins writing in French.
1946–1947	Highly creative period of writing in French produces novel, stories,

	and a play, none of which are published.
1947	Beginning of "siege in the room": writes *Molloy*.
1947–1948	Writes *Malone Meurt* (Malone Dies).
1948–1949	Writes *En Attendant Godot* (Waiting for Godot).
1949–1950	Writes *L'Innommable* (The Unnamable).
1950	Beckett's mother dies.
1950–1952	Writes *Textes pour Rien* (Texts for Nothing).
1951	*Malloy* and *Malone Meurt*, first two novels of the trilogy, published in Paris.
1952	*En Attendant Godot* published in Paris.
1953	First staging of *En Attendant Godot* at Théâtre de Babylone on Left Bank in Paris.
1955–1956	Writes *Fin de Partie* (Endgame).

1958	Writes *Krapp's Last Tape*.
1960	Writes *Comment C'est* (How It Is).
1961	Marries Suzanne Deschevaux-Dumesnil at Folkestone in England.
1964	Flies to New York for making of *Film* with Buster Keaton.
1969	Awarded Nobel Prize for Literature.
1972	First production of *Not I*.
1974	Writes *Old Earth*.
1989	Death of Beckett at age eighty-three.

Recommended Reading

Deirdre Bair, *Samuel Beckett* (Harcourt Brace Jovanovich, 1978). The first of the comprehensive biographies of Beckett that appeared during his lifetime. Captures a good picture of Beckett and is filled with fascinating details—though a few of these have been found to be factually incorrect. Unlike the larger biographies that followed after his death, this is at all times readable and can with no difficulty be absorbed from start to finish.

Samuel Beckett, *The Collected Shorter Plays* (Grove Press, 1984). All the lesser-known dramatic works, in which Beckett was often at his most experimental. Some work exceptionally well, others less well, but there is invariably something of interest to be found in even the most fugitive "dramaticules."

John Calder, *The Philosophy of Samuel Beckett* (Calder Publications, 2002). This unusual book by the faithful publisher of Beckett's prose in English benefits from the long friendship between the author and its subject. It also benefits from many remarks—gnomic and more expansive— that Beckett made in conversation. Some of its views are certainly controversial, but in being so they are also provocative as original thoughts about what Beckett was doing.

John Calder, ed., *A Samuel Beckett Reader* (Calder and Boyars, 1967). A good selection of Beckett's prose work. It ranges from *More Pricks Than Kicks* through to his last short prose pieces. The pieces are well chosen, and each contains a brief and informative introduction. By far the best way to sample Beckett's oeuvre before plunging into the work of your choice.

Ruby Cohn, *Samuel Beckett: The Comic Gamut* (Rutgers, 1962). Another critical classic, which succeeds in being both entertaining and insightful. Living up to its subtitle, the chapters run from "portrait of the artist as an old bum" to "a comic complex and a complex comic."

Anthony Cronin, *Samuel Beckett: The Last Modernist* (Da Capo, 1999). This lengthy labor of love covers in painstaking detail the long and wayward life of its subject. Cronin's role as a leading figure on the Dublin literary scene through much of Beckett's life makes him highly aware of what Beckett gained from his Irish background, as well as what he sought to escape from.

Hugh Kenner, *A Reader's Guide to Samuel Beckett* (Syracuse University Press, 1996). A classic critical work on Beckett, covering all the main masterpieces. Hugh Kenner knew Beckett personally and was one of his most penetrating and insightful critics. Contains many fascinating details and speculations.

James Knowlson, *Damned to Fame: The Life of Samuel Beckett* (Simon and Schuster, 1996). This exhaustive and occasionally exhausting work is over 850 pages. It is the result of many years of superb scholarship and covers as many of the facts as are available. Apart from length, the only drawback is that the American author sometimes misses the nuances of Beckett's quintessential European—Irish and French—life.

Index

A NOTE ON THE AUTHOR

Paul Strathern has lectured in philosophy and mathematics and now lives and writes in London. He is the author of the enormously successful series Philosophers in 90 Minutes. A Somerset Maugham Prize winner, he is also the author of books on history and travel, as well as five novels. His articles have appeared in a great many publications, including the *Observer* (London) and the *Irish Times*.

Paul Strathern's 90 Minutes series in philosophy, also published by Ivan R. Dee, includes individual books on Thomas Aquinas, Aristotle, St. Augustine, Berkeley, Confucius, Derrida, Descartes, Dewey, Foucault, Hegel, Heidegger, Hume, Kant, Kierkegaard, Leibniz, Locke, Machiavelli, Marx, J. S. Mill, Nietzsche, Plato, Rousseau, Bertrand Russell, Sartre, Schopenhauer, Socrates, Spinoza, and Wittgenstein.